When Ground Doves Fly

When Ground Doves Fly

Poems by

Esther Phillips

Ian Randle Publishers
Kingston ● *Miami*

First published in Jamaica, 2003 by
Ian Randle Publishers
11 Cunningham Avenue
Box 686, Kingston 6

ISBN 976-637-136-9 paperback

A catalogue record of this book is available from the
National Library of Jamaica

and in the United States by
Ian Randle Publishers, Inc

ISBN 0-9729358-5-1 paperback

© Esther Phillips

www.ianrandlepublishers.com

Cover design by Errol Stennett
Book design by Shelly-Gail Cooper

Illustrations by Marian Armitage

This book is dedicated to:

the Master Craftsman;
the memory of my grandmother, Louise;
my mother – woman of strength –
and all the matriarchs of the past
who molded me into shaping words.

Contents

Acknowledgements

For their unwavering support, I wish to thank my mother, my siblings: Andy, Uriel, Althia, Marian (Judith), Henry and Sherroll.

I wish to thank Judith in particular for her beautiful illustrations of the poems, and Sherroll for her ready and sympathetic ear. I thank my daughter, Simone, for bringing to my life and to my writing a special kind of significance.

Many thanks to Ian Randle Publishers, to Lisa Morgan and Arlene Hanson and all the other members of the Editorial and Marketing team. I am forever grateful for the encouragement of all my teachers, professors, friends and colleagues who helped to make this publication possible.

Working Hands

You do not like my hands;
working hands, you call them,
not a poet's, and its true
these hands have done perhaps
more than their share of chores.
But there is more:
these working hands have come
by clinging from cliff's edges,
from grasping broken ends of dreams
I held too long,
yet could not keep;
juggling with life,
striving to catch its angles
that sometimes cut too deep.
I tried to hold my world
that would not stay in place,
until I learnt to feel inside these hands
the grooves that fit,
so I could turn the wheel
for just another day,
sometimes another minute.
The callous grows to shield
the bruised and tender part:
let these hands tell you something
of a poet's art.

Morning Glory

Who else sees the small blue heart
in the white-edged flower,
the yellow 'early-lates',
orchid-blossoms on tamarind trees?
They don't see the red cotton flower
– turning to gold –
I saw when the first pod broke!

Shallot seasons up the morning air,
potato-slips catch silver
from telephone wires,
black-birds sing and diffuse
the white light.

I shout when I'm alone
and swing my arms and laugh
but when I see them coming,
I keep my joy inside,
and make believe
it's just another morning.

Dove Song

'Yuh hear dem doves? Somebody gwine home
to duh Maker soon.' (Granny)

I do not like this mourning
of the dove,
that darkens dawn
and mocks at love.
I like the quickness
of the sparrow's chirp,
the brisk blackbird's song.

I do not like
this contrapuntal error,
a cleft, in the mind's peace;
a slowing of the heart
against the will,
against light on lime trees,
the brightness of the red hibiscus.

This persistence of discord,
a swelling sadness,
too close
not far away.
This dove mourning
broken olive branches,
forsaken ark.
This dove mourning,
calling, calling....

Flight Home

See how the silenced engines
of the aeroplane
reverence this island.
Here is too much
of the depth of memories,
each one a sacrament.

Chalice
of aquamarine water,
reefs, like white
embroidered hems of priests,
murmuring
syllables of peace.

It is the heart's right
to hoard the place
it knows as home;
to guard its anguished love
against the curious eyes,
of those who seek it only as a paradise.

Poised above this land
I feel an Empire crumble
in the distance.

But here, black-birds sing
crickets chorus
doves cry, sparrows call,
sunset gilds a
            white-winged egret
                  gliding
                        homeward.

Sketch Before Nightfall

While the light nestles down
in purple flowers,
filters through wing-flight,
I walk beside this lake.
Here is no path for locusts;
nothing at the water's edge
invites them.

Only a blue heron stands watching
the building's reflection
as if wondering
how it floats on water,
while the black-footed egret,
S-bent into patience,
waits for the sluggish worm
to lift its head.

Mallard ducks dip,
sun rays slip
from palm leaves
to the lake's graying surface.

When the brown dove sounds
its evening call
on a falling breeze,
Chaos lies down,
twisting her hair
to the roots of trees and sleeps.

Colour Miami Caribbean

I could almost believe
this lake is azure;
brown bird swish-
ing over water
a flying-fish in flight,
bright scales
startling the sunlight.

Why hoards the grass its green
against grey water,
leaving no smile at the rocks' edge,
no emerald tint
gracing pale butterflies?
Is a prism locked
in the coot's red beak,
a bottle-brush tree,
caught in a cluster of coconuts?

Then one evening,
up leaps the light
flinging rainbows
through the fountain,
hurls a Bajan sunset
against Miami sky.

Island Harmony

We should have plucked the soft green from the hills
and snatched the blueness from the midday sky;
stolen perfumes out of the air that filled
limola trees and drenched the fields nearby.
We could have etched forever in our brains
the island's song, its deepest harmony
that echoed through the nights of summer rains
or hummed in rivers running to the sea.
So sure we were all shadows had their suns
and beauty would not seek to end itself,
that we did not do all we should have done
to store the varied joys of nature's wealth.
But if we'd had them all, some future dawn
Time would undo our hands; we'd find them gone.

Simonespeak

I'm glad for this time that you have found
for fifty-odd pages of poetry,
but before you get your volume bound,
where is your poem for me?

I know you have written at least one poem
for the one who claims he's your husband to be.
But surely your love is not all for him.
Where is your poem for *me*?

Your father, grandmother, sister and brother
are all in your pages of poetry.
And I, your precious and only daughter –
Not even *one* poem for me?

I'm planning to write a novel, Mom,
(It runs in the blood, you see)
I'll not ignore you in my book,
Oh no, *Mother dear*, not me.

I'll fill my pages with nothing but you,
for the whole universe to see
what's patently wrong with Mums who exclude
their daughters from their poetry.

Grandmother's Crosses

I

My Grandmother's hands
were full of crosses –
her seven grandchildren, to be exact
(our mother had migrated).
Gran never flinched, just waited
for the morning cloud to break,
then she was planting,
digging yams, potatoes,
eddoes, increase peas,
so seven mouths would not go hungry.

She knew the secrets of the woods
and she followed,
trekking through a nearby gully,
picking circe bush, bitter as gall,
to cure colds;
bush-ball, vermifuge
to 'purge out de system';
gully-root to soothe woman pain.

She took her produce to town
on the six o'clock bus,
selling among the sweat and market stench,
then waited in the bus-stand,
basket on head, to come home.
And I in high-school uniform,
waited with her

(standing at a distance),
pleats and young pride stiffened,
one with the starch of cassava
she had squeezed, grated, peeled
with her own hands.

II

Then shame gave way to love
and I scrambled for a seat
and yelled for Gran to come
so she could rest her weary feet.

By lamplight she talked
of her 'young girl' days:
she had picked pond grass
for ten cents a day,
gathered dry sticks
to make cooking fire,
run from the overseer
who felt that his hire
included the right
to 'interfere' with her.
We knew of her conversion,
kneeling, weeping
in a Mission Hall,
when Jesus came
and never left her heart.

In time, my grandmother shared
the Triumph of the cross,
each one of the seven.

This one teaching,
others working in Government,
… going to University:
'Dey all do good wid de help o' de Lord,
I too proud o' all muh pickney'.

III

Today I looked at the Cross
leading my grandmother's casket
and thought of those
that she had carried in her hands …

'Please Granny, turn this call backwards
Mark your turpentine cross at the door
Turn my blue nightgown inside-out
Chant a psalm, a prayer
to protect me from the lurking heart-man,
from haig-ridden nights,
the wrong turning at crossroads …'

That this young man, the Crucifer,
now moving down the aisle,
should bear this Cross
with such indifferent calm
perhaps was right.
Folding her thumb inside her palm
before she died,
Gran had relinquished all.

They say I have my Grandmother's hands.
I shape my crosses:
in Words.

Grandmother On Track

Smell of ripe sugar-cane,
fragrant limola,
frangipani blossoms
wafting through
a light-blue Bajan air...

Striding on the cold green asphalt,
I pushed these memories
inside my track-suit pocket ...
then she was there.

Didn't want to pass too quickly,
thought of it too late,
feared my pace would seem to mock
her slow, rocking gait.

Waves pounding rocks at Consett Bay,
morning moon over Bathsheba,
days maddened by too much sunlight
and blackbirds' ceaseless clamor.

Second time around the track
she tapped me sharply on the back:
'Those nubian knots, young lady,
they look very, very good'.
My answer didn't seem to matter,
'Don't forget. *Don't forget*',
she said –
as if I could.

I Do Not Know My Father

I keep wanting to meet my father,
I do not know who he is;
I know of the smooth
smart-talking, impossible dreamer
my mother speaks about.

I remember a man
planing wood in the back-yard –
where I longed to play
in the shavings that fell –
who hopped on his bicycle
and left;
those days when anger,
spewed out from my mother,
ran like lava through the house
and all around it.

I know the man I saw years after,
who tried to fit words into pictures of the past,
and did not know the pictures, memories, words
were warped out of all meaning,
frames twisted out of joint.

I heard him speak
of the glory of God
and the power of angels
and the saving grace that kept him
through the long years

of cold rooms
and alien faces.

But I do not know my father,
I do not know what is behind
the skilled words, and sometimes
loud and reckless laughter,
(Time whittled to a prop
 to fit the stage,
'till my two-week holiday is over).

I had no clues
when goodbye came
to help me gauge the truth of his embrace,
but I look back, and dare to think
that it was grief I saw,
etched on his face.

Aunt Lill

It is by smells I remember you best –
an ancient dome-topped cedar chest

covered by camphor-scented woolen shawls.
Inside, fragrant in dried khus-khus, shiny mothballs,

white tablecloths bordered by intricate
embroidery; hand towels and linens immaculate.

Figs in a cold stone-floor pantry,
drying sea-moss, bottles of guava jelly.

Pears and mangoes ripening in an old store-room.
Smell of coconut bread on a sunny afternoon.

Gone – Another year this Easter time, and I remember
You, named for lilies and the scents that linger.

Half Measures

You come to me saying
half a loaf is better than none at all.
But when your half a loaf
sticks in the gullet
choking out tears,
leaves a hungry belly
tricked for a while with crumbs,
then it's better
you take your half a loaf home
and leave me nothing.

Out of nothing,
I *must* create.

Eva's Dilemma

You can't guess a woman's loneliness
when sex is not enough,
and she lies, wrapped
in pink-striped silence,
eyes averted with what he thinks is anger.
'You don't enjoy it very much
any more, do you?'
'Yes, but...'
How to explain?

The trouble wasn't only
Adam's eating of the apple,
but that he hadn't thought to do it
from the very start.
So he still comes
after the fact;
the thrust into a core
that he does not comprehend.

And her softly out-stretched hand
lingers in the dull vibration
of his snores –
deep in sleep,
he does not dream
of his dead seed
on her naked thigh,
nor touch the crushed rails
of her heart's high altar.

17

Seashells

Across the broken spectrum
of a seagull's cry,
your face comes back to me
half sketched in sunset.
I've always loved collecting shells.
I picked up so many as a boy.

You, the curious mixture:
all scientist, careful of detail;
the artist, who loves those days
you call *seeing,* when even a rusty nail is brilliant,
and the hair on your arms
stands straight at the way
the light falls over Bathsheba
and casuarinas shape themselves
against the sky.

I've seen how you brush sand
gently off the shells,
how your fingers trace them,
caress the smooth inner whorls.
It tells me you feel every fissure,
every healed-over scar.

Touch this tender strain;
let my music rise again
clearer than bird-cry,
sweeter than the ocean-song
a seashell never loses.

Bluesy Poem

Walk against the sun
...not into it...
so she always played
in shadows,
walked cloudy days
or in the rain;
her colours were never
sunshine yellows,
electric blues or reds,
only muted shades –
dark browns or grays.

 When he strode into her life
– giant that he was –
his shadow became
her circumference,
she could be anything
she wanted (in silhouette):
thin as a paper doll
flat against the wall
when he wanted
his space,
grow huge arms
if he needed
mother-comfort.

Tired of
mouldy walls
and echoes

he left her
walking straight
into the sun

tired of
mouldy walls
and echoes
he left her
walking out
into the sun.

*Paso Doble

'With this partner I feel nothing.'
Sweet Anodyne!
A flick of a CD player
and he's the matador.

He treads so lightly over guilt,
spins deftly over a dilemma;
She, his red cloak,
sweet anodyne.

So wave your cloak, proud matador,
She stands between you
and the bull.
Balance your weight
on the balls of your feet,
Sur Place, Deplacement,
Wave your red cloak
from left to right,
from one side to another,
and let the bull pursue her.

See how she tries to follow
    your double step!
your false step!
    two-timing step!
So the horns of the bull
will pierce her,
and the red of the cloak
will be scattered.

No more cloaks for the asking,
for you've stripped and torn
all you've had.

Now it's you and the bull,
matador,
Just you
and the Bull!

* The Paso Doble is a Latin dance. Translated, the name means 'double step'. The male dancer is the matador and the female partner represents the red cloak or cape waved by the matador.

Requiem For A Lover

Other graves I have kept closed,
careless of the weeds un-naming them,
but yours I wanted to open.
They say a ghost will yield up its secrets
kept from the living.
So I lay aside your grave-clothes,
stroked my finger softly on your cheek,
the way I did sometimes
when you were half-asleep.

Tell me, in this half-dream state
why your heart faltered;
or was it always only like the winged bird
fluttering spaces in twilight,
unsure of its homing?

I had tuned my ears
to songs of the wind,
had learnt their cadences,
and smiled when promised symphonies
were merely rustlings along a drying palm leaf.

But you were the resonance of thunder;
you dared spaces to be anything but empty,
hiding with such care your sacred vows
within my hollow places.

Till I no longer danced
on the moon's thin edge,
but was the moon herself,
full, replete,
cracks of tension
now a smooth unbroken surface,
luminous with sun and earth-shine.

Tell me, why did your heart falter,
like the full tide receding,
laying no claim to the shore
to which it had raced;
retreating, thin as gossamer
on grains of sand?

If I should pitch a star
to the end of the world
I could not wake you.

So I cross your hands over your chest,
and pray the folding wings
hasten the bird's flight homeward.

May the rain, on this grave,
be gentle.

Closure

I knew the day would come,
when the bright crimson of you would fade,
and I would ask the wind your name
and it would scarcely answer,
if at all.

I knew I'd walk this beach again,
find a shell, some piece of seaweed
that bore no imprint of your hands, your face.

I hear the ocean sing in aqua
marine-gue off deep blue chords
close on a white whisper.

No physics of motion;
no little-boy tales you told a thousand times
(as still you do, no doubt)
of how you'd swim far out,
against your mother's pleas,
indifferent, even then.

Dawn grows more tender
with your absence,
the dragonfly stilled.

You said it could not happen,
but last evening, all alone,
I saw the brilliant flash of green at sunset,
and in that moment,
knew how the dying of one love
awakens another,
then looking eastward,
knew why a rainbow,
streaking emerald,
arced outward.

Steal Away

(During their secret meetings, the slaves had a practice of speaking over a pot of water in order to muffle the sounds of their prayers).

sing in a whispuh
steal away
don't let 'im hear yuh
when yuh pray
come in de circle
bend right ovuh
drop yuh sorrow
into de watuh.
When yuh rage unleash
and yuh feel yuh mus' shout
don't let 'im hear yuh
cover yuh mout'
breathe it into de watuh
let de heat in yuh brain
rise up like de mist
and soothe like de rain
speak it low in de watuh
let de Spirit hear
tell 'im yuh pray
dat deliv'rance near
sing in a whispuh
steal away
don't let 'im hear yuh
he kill yuh next day.

Poet Anansi[1]

I am the Trickster,
I spin shadow in light,
Master of chiaroscuro,
neither black nor white.
My webbed fingers
whittle words from stone,
sculpt them from bone,
wrest them from spirit.

I am the Trickster
You the chased,
I am not tender
when I embrace:
I tease your tongue to madness
with the salt of words,
squeeze images through veins,
pluck them from protest.

I am the Trickster
With silken thread glistening
I beguile you to rough places,
yet you follow,
for you know me:
Interpreter of voices,
Spinner of sacred visions
at midnight.
In your mother's womb
I cauled[2] you,
gave you second sight.

1. *Anansi is the Trickster figure of African and Caribbean folklore. He is represented in the form of a spider, and is known for his clever tricks and deceptive dealings. Anansi is the guardian of crossroads. He is also the Interpreter.*
2. *A caul is a web-like membrane covering the faces of infants at birth; supposedly containing mystical powers.*

For The Children Drowned In The Middle Passage

I said that they were not
my children when I felt their spongy fingers
tugging at my breasts.
Then they slipped away.
I never heard their footsteps:
soles soaked too soon in ocean brine
can make no sound – I never met their eyes.

Now, I call the ancestors to come,
crowd around my birth-stool;
circle the ocean,
bind the scattering wind.

Keeper of Waters,
Friend of the Fatherless,
Interpreter of every lamentation,
free the children's voices
strangled in seaweed,
that I may birth
their tribal songs.

Lament For Maureen

What words, what images
best fit the shape of grief?
What song?
What skillful rendering
bring relief from memory?

Too soon. Too soon
the stilling of a gentle voice,
a heart grown weary:
sparrow wounded by wind-shear
whirling, fluttering,
falling, broken bones.
No tender breeze
to bring you safely home.

So we who love you
gather you,
we make a nesting place here,
just a while, for you,

we bring you words
in softened syllables
to soothe,
perfume in flowers
to delight you,
salt tears
to heal your wounds.

Come, North Wind,
bearer of birds heavenward,
there is the Lover of her soul
Who waits for her.
Take her to Him, quickly.
But bear her,
gently.

Prayer For A Surfer

(inspired by a bumper sticker: 'Pray for Surf')

Meet him, I ask You,
on a wave;
speak to him in the whirling wind
and roaring of the ocean's thunder.
Let him hear You
from the centre of the wave,
where every sound
is perfect stillness.
O tell him
it's not skill alone
that keeps him
from the ocean's harms,
but underneath him, always,
are Your everlasting arms.

Just Riffing

Sometimes I get frighten'
that I losing my true rhythm:
like if I standing still
outside my heart,
hearing it beating
in iambic metre,
unrhymed trimetre.

When I feel I hearing kaiso
bursting through Miami palm trees,
steel-pan sweet like cane juice
rippling through the evening breeze,
my heart want to leap like RPB lyrics,
flow strong and smooth
as Gwyneth Squires doing the Sailor Dance.

But I holding it back
in quatrains,
end-stopped lines,
half-rhymes.

Look! I come from tuk-band land,
raga-soca land,
calypso country.
I come from a place
where we measure morning
by cocks crowing in backyards,
pick up rhythms in raindrops
drumming on galvanize' roof tops,

sense the length of a line
in the sighing of casuarinas.
We learn the harmony of syllables
singing through canefields,
hear women birthing
the spirit of Blues in Mission Halls.

I come from a place
where God borrow colours
from Eden days,
mix them with crystal water
nearest the Throne,
then pour them 'cross the sky
over Bathsheba, for sunrise.

This is a place where the foam
over reefs as white as the bones
of my ancestors,
the green of the sea
is the grief of memory
and gladness of limola trees
in brilliant sunlight.
We learn a day's diminuendo
in the flight of a firefly,
the chorus of crickets
on rainy evenings.

But for now,
I just here meterizing
metaphorizing
just improvising

just riffin'.

Woman In The Moon

Man, thinking he was first,
commissioned himself to the moon
and landed, of all places, on maria[1]!
Maria Imbrium[2]
smooth from a distance,
dark as the seas
for which the ancients named her.
Maria Imbrium
Sea of Showers
Sea of tears
shaped by collision
moulded by meteors of men.

Maria Nubium,
she of the Straight Wall,
broken,
holding the scorch of lava
in her belly.
Melting, fragmented,
she forms her valleys
in strain and stress;
births mountains
against the bright highlands.

Maria Serenitatis,
mysterious, wise,
knowing that impact is creation;
that this night's crescent

curbing the void,
will come to fullness
in its season.

Maria Imbrium
Maria Nubium
Maria Serenitatis
still birthing generations
still bearing up men
still cool under pressure,
knowing how to make
the bitter crust of lava,
sweet.

Luminescent
Brilliant
Abundant
Beneficent
Blessed are you, Maria
Blessed are you.

1.   *Maria are landing sites for astronauts on the moon. These areas were thought to be
     waters or seas.*
2.   *Imbrium, Nubium and Serenitatis are names given to maria.*

Girl On The Metro

'Don't leave me.'
I looked at her, heart quickening.
She rushed from the door,
leaned against the seat,
long shuddering sobs,
palm outward stretched.
'Don't leave me.'
But her eyes: not one tear,
just wide, clear as the sea.

The Metro aisle became her stage;
her ally, the train's rhythmic rattle.
She sang in high-pitched treble
her special version of 'soh rey me doh'
gave an update of the weather,
played a clown, an angel
on her own metro show.

What world did she inhabit?

Some twelve-year-olds
still wear their hair in plaits,
but hers was done in lavish style
piled up high, sprayed to metallic stiffness.

Had someone grown impatient
and had already marked her?
What awful night
had robbed this young girl
of her tears; and locked her tight
inside her daydreams?

Illusion

It's not that I did not feel
your pain, Sisters,
your words and wounds
were mine.
It's not that I didn't
once feel my destiny
pulsing through
my own fingertips.
I have, you'll say,
exchanged one cross for another:
the wound of the heart
for the thrust of the spear —
but those *green lights*
led me to a place
where pain grew out of pavements,
and truths were neither
red nor green
but always faltering somewhere
in between,
and window-dressing
was a thousand dark chimeras.

Epiphany

I am almost tempted sometimes
to slip quietly,
unobtrusively
into that feeling that you get
when you've looked into a mirror
for a very long time,
and the image you've grown used to
blurs
and, for a moment,
you become something
that eludes you
and you're never
the same again.

Or when you sit
in a darkened church
and, for a fleeting moment,
the glow that you see
is the light of the Cross.

Or when you stand alone by the sea
and hear a different
orchestration of sound,
and only your body remains
on the sand, like a sea-shell,
and whatever it is in you
that vibrates to the music of life
is out there in the middle
somewhere.

Or when you hover
between sleep and wake
and your spirit,
freed by the body's restfulness,
takes flight, and what you see
is clearer than vision
or thought.

I am tempted sometimes
to slip quietly beyond
this existence,
which lies merely
between the Truth
and the darkness,
the half-light and the Light.

Something In Us
(for Lorna Goodison)

Something in us is often lonely,
ready to pick its way across debris
grown too familiar,
and hook on to the star
we recognise as ours.

Something in us turns over
after the best love-making,
and gazes where a grasshopper
leaps against the moon.

Something in the ocean's roar,
light tremulous, dancing on water;
some dim memory in the angle
of the sea-gull's wing, the lift,
the curve of a bird's soaring.

We cling too close to earth
and all but die;
Why do ground-doves walk
when they can fly?

Wall

Not the Empire State Building,
Statue of Liberty, Ground Zero;
not all the famous landmarks
for which the eye might scan
a New York night-scape.

I'm looking for a wall
somewhere in Brooklyn,
the one my father built:
a high wall, a very long wall.
I heard the slow thud
of concrete, the clang
of steel girding its foundation;
I heard it settling
all across the Atlantic ocean.

This wall repeats itself
in bricks of twelve:
a father, mother, seven children alive,
two never brought to birth,
one dead, un-named.
These are the stones in the wall
of my father's wailing,
his bitter regret, his shame.

His was a dream of wide pastures,
rimless horizons. He, a young David –
lion conqueror, defeater of giants,
betrayed by the strength of his own loins.
No vine dresser, tending the fruit
he bore too early;

saying goodbye, he left
and built, instead, a wall in Brooklyn city.

Daddy, Daddy, come to the wall
Listen a moment, hear when I call
I'm not made of brick
and I'm not made of stone
I cried all those nights
when you never came home
I've figured out ways
I might climb up the wall
but your wall is too high
and I'm scared I might fall
and there's no one to catch me
there never has been
just the earth and the sky
and nothing between

Listen, Daddy, hear me call …

Daddy… Daddy …

I wait by the wall.

Filling Space(s)

What strange Muse taught me
how to fill the spaces
of his silence?
A Child of Nature,
I abhorred the vacuum,
the obdurate nothingness
that followed a quarrel,
or sometimes filled the house
for no apparent reason.

And so, one day,
when my heart raged
for any kind of resonance;
my fingers longed to sculpt
some form that I could christen
his, or mine, or ours,
She came, this Muse.

The very next day,
I shaped his silence
into soft summer rain,
I, the frangipani,
Bright heart cupped
to tenderest drops,
yielding, petals unfurling.

One July evening, when we walked at Consett Bay,
I grabbed a corner of his silence
before it settled

and we were off, far
off in the ocean's centre.

Strong, silent giant,
he hurled from the ocean bed
the jagged boulders, so they
would not cause me injury;
I couldn't slip from the curling
edge of a wave; he caught me.
And when he spoke again,
(not till some three days later)
I swore his lips still dripped
the salt tang of the sea.

Until I learnt
how skilled he was
in filling his own spaces:
No Muse,
no otherworldly inspiration,
just flesh and blood –
the Other Woman
their children, his, and hers.

I give you back your space,
your silences.
And claim my own.
How strange that I,
dreading the years' nothingness
am now adept
at naming silences,
shaping spaces.

Mine still the bright heart
cupped, open
to rain and sun, and wind,
to galaxies emerging,
stellar explosions
I may fashion as I choose.
I, 'Sister planet',
refractory, vast,
in crescent phase more brilliant
than a thousand wheeling stars.

Lightning Source UK Ltd.
Milton Keynes UK
UKHW020616281122
412969UK00009B/1558